Wilderness Album Series
INVERTEBRATES
Nature stories for children

Author and Illustrator
Barbara Batulla
Entomologist

*The author wishes to thank Dr. F. S. Ward,
Dr. M. Samoiloff, Dr. C. Aitchison, Dr. C. Jay,
Dr. T. Galloway, and Dr. Hartwick for
technical advice and assistance. Special
thanks to Dr. R. Wrigley.*

**All conversions from metric to imperial are
averaged.**

A Sterling/Hyperion book
© 1990 Hyperion Press Limited

Sterling Publishing Co., Inc.
387 Park Avenue South, New York, NY 10016

Produced by Hyperion Press Limited
300 Wales Avenue, Winnipeg, MB, Canada R2M 2S9
ISBN: 0-920534-57-0
Distributed in Canada by Sterling Publishing
c/o Canadian Manda Group
P.O. Box 920, Station U, Toronto, Ontario
M8Z 5P9 Canada

Printed in U.S.A.

CONTENTS

The Wilderness Album Series includes nature stories for children plus scientific information and line drawings. Titles in the wildlife series include *Vanishing Animals, Extinct Animals, Tropical Birds, Venomous Animals, Animals of the Dark, Animal Invaders, Small Mammals, Large Mammals* Vols. I and II, *Birds* Vols. I and II, *Owls in North America, Insects. Butterflies and Moths, Fish, Time and Life* (Fossils), *Wildflowers, Trees, Wild Edibles, Invertebrates, Reptiles and Amphibians, Dinosaurs.*

Protozoan

The tiny euglena (you-glee-na) zoomed through the water using its flagellum (flaw-jell-um) like a propeller. Every so often it zoomed this way or that to capture some floating particle. The euglena had organs in its body called chloroplasts (klor-o-plasts) which helped it turn light energy from the sun, carbon dioxide, and water into edible food energy as plants do.

The euglena was not the only microscopic creature out shopping for lunch, so it had to be careful that it did not become someone else's meal. A ferocious peranema (pear-a-nee-ma) could be hiding among the microscopic plants and algae. All the euglena had to do was cast a shadow over the peranema's light-sensing organ or accidentally touch the peranema's flagella and a deadly race would be on!

Even on the pond floor danger was lurking. There the euglena could fall into the sticky grasp of an amoeba (a-mee-baa) or its cousin the shelled amoeba, both of which had long arm-like pseudopods (sue-doe-pods) that could start to digest the euglena on the first touch. But the most dangerous enemy of all was the paramecium (pear-a-mee-see-um). These amazing hunters were not only the swiftest of the protozoa, they were also the deadliest! With one sweeping pull, a paramecium could easily draw the slower moving euglena into its mouth. If the euglena tried to escape, the paramecium could shoot and paralyze it using barbed arrow-like trichocysts (try-coe-cists) located near the entrance to its mouth.

Just then a paramecium appeared from out of the algae. The euglena sensed its movement with the light-sensing organ at the base of its flagellum and instinctively moved away from the danger. Either the paramecium did not notice the euglena, or else it had its sensory cilia (hairs) set on easier prey. It spiraled right past the euglena and attacked a slower moving three-armed ceratium nearby. The euglena had been very lucky. While the paramecium fought with its hard-shelled victim, the euglena quickly swam for cover and safety.

Phylum   Protozoa
Class   Phytomastigophora (euglena, peranema, ceratium),
Class   Filosa (amoeba), *Class*   Ciliatea (paramecium)
Size   Most species are microscopic, the average size being about .1 mm (.004 in).
Distribution   The protozoa are a very large group of one-celled animals found throughout the world. Most live in freshwater, saltwater, or in the soil. Some live as parasites within other animals' bodies.
Food   Diet varies from one species to another. Euglena and other primitive species can make much of their own food. Amoeba, paramecium, and peranema eat other animals, while some species eat both plant and animal material. To capture food, euglena and peranema surround food particles in a deep pocket in the body wall, the edges of which close up around their food. The food and the pocket, called a vacuole (vac-you-oal), are then drawn inside the protozoan's body and enzymes are secreted into the vacuole to digest the food.

Peranema may also use its rod organ (thickened rod to which the second flagellum is attached) as an anchor to pull in prey or to suck juices from the prey's body. Amoebas and radiolarians capture their food using long arm-like pseudopods which are covered in a sticky mucous containing digestive enzymes that begin to digest prey on first contact. After the prey is completely coated, the protozoan draws it into its body, completing digestion within a vacuole. The ciliates, including paramecium, actually have a mouth-like opening called a buccal (b-you-cal) cavity which is coated with tiny hairs that draw in food particles.

Life History   It is difficult to say how long individual protozoans live because they are always dividing. Division or asexual reproduction is the most common method of reproduction during favorable weather and occurs when one individual protozoan divides or duplicates itself to produce an identical twin. A second method, sexual reproduction, occurs regularly only in more advanced species, not in euglena, ceratium, or peranema, and only rarely in amoebas. In the simplest method of sexual reproduction, two protozoa join together and exchange material from within their nuclei (the message centre of their bodies). The two protozoa then separate and divide.

At some time in their lives most protozoa face winter, drought, or some other weather change. At that time some species may use another method of sexual reproduction. Others sink to the bottom and form a protective coating or cyst which protects them until more favorable conditions exist.

Comments   The protozoa vary greatly in form, lifestyle, and diet. Some species, like euglena, have one or more flagella which help them swim through the water. Others such as paramecium have tiny hairs called cilia which move in rhythm causing the animal to flow through the water. Still others have beautiful protective cases or shells on their bodies and move on foot-like pseudopods. Some protozoa are parasites of other animals.

Color of protozoa
Most of the protozoa are clear or opaque, taking on the color of their surroundings. The euglena (centre of picture) is bright green. Peranema (centre right) and amoeba (bottom left) are clear whitish-green, ceratium (below peranema) is light yellowish-brown, the shelled (bottom right) amoeba has clear arms and a light reddish shell while the paramecium (top left) is clear to light green.

Freshwater Sponge

The lake was a good place to live, still clear, deep, and cold in the middle and shallow and warm along the edges. It was home to many creatures including a population of freshwater sponges. Many of these sponges lived in or near the mouth of a stream that flowed into the lake. There, the water was rich in nutrients and moving fast enough to make food capture easy for the sponges.

One sponge was attached to an old log in a hollow away from direct currents. It had started the season in an over-wintering bud called a gemmule and through the weeks of spring it grew and branched out along the log. Its skeleton of spongy fibres and sharp spicules was very delicate, but because it was living in a more sheltered spot than some of the other sponges it had been able to grow larger lobe-like branches. Each of these lobes was a grassy green color due to algae (microscopic plants) that were living within its own cells. By cooperating with this algae, the sponge could blend in with its surroundings so that enemies would not notice it.

Sponges do not have special body organs as higher animals do, but that does not mean that the little sponge could not feed itself. As a fresh stream of water entered its pool, the sponge pores opened a little wider. Inside the pores, many tiny cells called choanocytes (koe-an-o-sites), with cone-like collars, began to beat their whip-like tails or flagella. The combined motion of the tails of the choanocyte cells caused a current which drew water and food particles into the pores and down long passageways or canals, leading eventually to the centre of the sponge. Some of the food particles in the current hit the sides of the canal walls and were captured by the choanocytes and then transferred to other amoeba-like cells. These amoeba-like cells then digested the food and carried it into the inner tissues of the sponge to feed other cells. The sponge needed a great deal of food because it was feeding not only itself but also an egg that was growing inside it. When the time was right, a young paramecium-like larva would form, separate itself from the mother's tissues, and slowly swim with the current through the maze of tunnels within its mother, towards an outside pore called an osculum. Then along with wastes and circulated water, it would be thrown out into the real world. The larva would then spend a few hours swimming about, searching for its own log or rock on which to spend the rest of its life. All the while it would have to be wary of all the creatures that would try to eat it. The young sponge would have many enemies on its road to maturity.

Phylum Porozoa

Class Demospongiae

Size Sponges vary greatly in size. Some marine species are as large as washtubs while others are no larger than a bean. Most freshwater sponges are smaller encrusting species that grow larger and more branched in calm waters than in areas with currents. The species in the story may grow to 26 cm (10 in) in length (along a branch or rock) and up to 2 cm (0.8 in) in thickness.

Distribution Of the 10,000 species of sponges found in the world, only 150 species live in freshwater lakes and streams (approximately 30 in North America). The species in the story is found in fresh clean waters no deeper than 2 m (6 ft) in lakes and ponds throughout Canada and the United States.

Food Sponges eat microscopic food particles, bacteria, and some protozoa. They capture food by drawing small currents of water into pores or holes in the sides of their bodies. The water current is caused by constantly moving flagella which are attached to cells lining the pore walls. Water drawn into the sponge eventually leaves along with waste products through a hole or holes called oscula. The food particles are trapped on the cell walls and digested by other amoeba-like cells which then carry the nutrients to other parts of the sponge.

Life History Sponges start their lives in one of three ways: as buds growing off the parent sponge, as overwintering gemmules, or as baby sponges or larvae that develop within the mother sponge from a fertilized egg.

Larvae are produced by sexual reproduction. Gemmules and buds are produced asexually. Buds and larvae may be produced anytime during the summer, but gemmules are often produced only in the autumn or during other times of environmental extremes. Gemmules are ball-like resting stages with a tough protective outer coating and softer live cells within. Once conditions become more favorable, the gemmules crack open and the sponge begins to grow again. Portions of an adult sponge can also survive the winter.

Comments Sponges can be grouped into 3 categories. The first group includes the common bath sponge. These are harvested from shallow coastal oceans for use in homes and bath sponges have a skeleton made of a flexible fiber-like tissue called spongin. Although freshwater sponges do not look or feel like bath sponges, they do belong to this group.

The second group, the glass sponges, live only in deep ocean waters from 450 to 900 m (1,500 - 3,000 ft). They have a hard skeleton made of microscopic glass-like spikes called spicules which interlock to form intricate lattice-like patterns.

The third type of sponge is the chalky or hard sponge. These ocean-dwelling sponges have calcium in their spicules and are often chalky or dull in appearance. Many are very small and most do not grow larger than 15 cm (6 in) in height.

Color of freshwater sponge
The sponge is bright grass-green. The larva is white with tiny green specks.

An in-current pore

Hydra

It was close to recess time but Valerie was not interested in playing today. As soon as the school bell rang, she was at the class aquarium, her nose pressed against the glass, peering into the murky water.

Two days before, her class had been on a field trip to a nearby marsh. There they had collected insects, frogs, and other aquatic life. When it was time to leave, they put everything back except for a few special creatures that Valerie's teacher allowed them to take back to class for further study. To create a home or habitat for their guests, the children also collected some sand and aquatic plants.

Valerie was amazed at the number of tiny animals that lived in the water. Some, like the paramecium, seemed to glide along. Others, like the rotifer, seemed to have their own little propellers. The most bizarre of all however, was the hydra. It was plant-like in appearance with a stem-like body and anchor at one end, and a mouth surrounded by four to six tentacles at the other end. Valerie could see two hydras — one resting on a plant, the other on the bottom of the aquarium. The one on the plant had a baby budding from its stalk. Valerie squinted hard, trying to get a better look at them. Her teacher was pleased by the girl's interest and brought her a magnifying glass.

"Try using this," she suggested.

"Wow, thanks Mrs. Wilson," said Valerie. Now she could see the hydra quite clearly. The one on the plant was sitting very still with its arms or tentacles outstretched. The tentacles on the budding hydra were not full grown and under magnification they looked like warty little bumps. The other hydra, on the aquarium floor, seemed to be stretched out in one direction as if trying to get a better look at something, but of course this could not be so because hydras do not have eyes. Valerie looked in the direction the hydra was bending and there she saw two tiny crustaceans (krus-tay-shuns) struggling over a morsel of food. Could it be that the hydra was hungry too? It seemed so, for within a matter of seconds the hydra let go its hold on the aquarium floor and did a somersault that brought it within a few millimeters of the unsuspecting crustaceans.

"Look at this!" cried Valerie, "The hydra just did a somersault. I think it's after the crustacean's food."

"I think it's after the crustacean, not its food," said Mrs. Wilson as she came over to the aquarium. "But we'll see."

As the hydra touched one of the crustaceans, a slight tremor went through its tentacles. The crustacean twitched as if in pain and began to weave and wobble as it tried to escape.

"What's happening I wonder?" said Valerie.

"The hydra has weapons on its tentacles called nematocysts (nee-ma-toe-sists). It can shoot these stings at its enemies or prey. Some are poisonous spears that penetrate and paralyze the victim's body. Others are like sticky long whips which wrap around the prey, tangling its legs and making escape difficult," explained Mrs. Wilson.

As they watched, the hydra grabbed the crustacean with its tentacles and stuffed the creature into its mouth.

Valerie groaned.

"Well, that's nature," responded her teacher.

Phylum   Cnidaria

Class   Hydrozoa

Size   Hydras range in size from 2 mm (.08 in) to 19 mm (0.8 in) or more in length.

Distribution   Hydras are found in freshwater lakes, marshes, and streams throughout the world.

Food   Hydras feed mainly on crustaceans and sometimes on other small aquatic invertebrates. The hydra captures its food using its tentacles which are armed with poisonous nematocysts. The nematocysts are whip-like coiled harpoons that either poison or wrap around prey, making escape difficult.

Life History   In cold regions, hydras overwinter in the egg stage surrounded by a protective covering. When spring arrives, the covering breaks down and a young hydra emerges and begins to grow. When it reaches a certain stage, it will grow buds that develop into new hydras. This continues until late summer. Then, as temperature and day length decrease, the hydra prepares for winter by producing either an ovary or testis on the side of its stalk. Sperm released from the testis of one hydra then swim in search of a hydra with an ovary. If one is found, the sperm fertilizes the egg inside the ovary, the egg develops a protective coating, and drops off the parent hydra to wait out winter on the pond floor. There are many generations per year. Lifespan is one year.

Comments   Hydras belong to the same group as the sea anemones, hydroids, corals, and jellyfish. To see some sea anemones, look at the octopus, sea cucumber, and cover pictures. Hydras, corals, sea anemones, and jellyfish all feed using tentacles armed with nematocysts. Like the hydra, they all have a simple body cavity — food enters from one opening, is digested, absorbed, and waste products leave from the same opening.

Hydras are named after a many-headed mythological Greek serpent called Hydra. According to legend, every time one of the serpent's heads was cut off, it grew two new ones in its place! Like its namesake, hydras are also able to regrow portions of their bodies (although not in doubles).

Color of hydra
Hydras vary in color depending on the species and what they have been eating. Hydras are pink, white, tan, brown, or green.

Jellyfish

The sea nettle jellyfish pulsed gracefully through the water. It moved by tightening and relaxing muscles around the edge of its soft bell-shaped body, making it smaller, then bigger, then smaller, just like an umbrella opening and closing. Every few minutes it would rest, letting the gentle ocean currents carry it along. Hanging down from its body were many harmless-looking streamers called tentacles. But harmless they were not, for along with four ribbon-like arms, these tentacles formed the defense and food-collecting systems of the jellyfish. Any small creature that accidentally came in contact with this gently swaying army of sticky strings would quickly be stung by hundreds of poisonous harpoon-like barbs called nematocysts and tangled up in the strings. These barbs were located on the edge of the bell, on the tentacles, and on the arms. Once a victim was dead, or at least paralyzed, the jellyfish would coil the tentacles, thus holding the creature up to its mouth for an easy meal. Food particles trapped on one of the jellyfish's four arms were also wiped across the mouth and digested in its large bag-like stomach.

The sea nettle was dangerous to larger animals too. In fact sea nettles have been known to give people some nasty stings. Amazingly this sea nettle had several small fish darting here and there between its tentacles and arms. For these fish, the stinging tentacles of the jellyfish served as protection from enemies. As long as the fish did not actually touch any part of the sea nettle, they remained unharmed and safe from their own enemies which were too large to find their way safely through the mass of arms and tentacles. The fish probably helped the sea nettle by dropping bits of food that the jellyfish could then catch in its tentacles.

Nearby, another jellyfish, a moon jelly, floated in a bed of algae. This jellyfish had no fish swimming around it. It had no long streaming tentacles either. In fact, it was rarely dangerous to larger animals. The moon jelly could move about as the sea nettle did, but for the most part it seemed to prefer just floating with the current, pulsing upward every so often to keep itself level. To catch food it merely allowed itself to sink slowly to the bottom — trapping small plants and animals underneath its sticky bell. Then the trapped food would be transferred to the moon jelly's mouth by sweeping one of its four arms across the bottom of the bell. Do you think this is a boring way of life? Would you want to be a jellyfish?

Phylum Cnidaria
Class Scyphozoa
Size Jellyfish range in size from 2 to 40 cm (1 to 16 in). One species grows up to 2 m (2 yds) in diameter. The sea nettle ranges from 10 to 25 cm (4 to 10 in) across, with 24 to 40 tentacles depending on its habitat (brackish water forms are smaller). The moon jellyfish grows up to 41 cm (16 in) across.

Distribution Jellyfish can be found in coastal waters from the Arctic to tropical seas. The sea nettle occurs from Cape Cod south to the West Indies. The moon jellyfish inhabits Arctic and Greenland waters. It has worldwide distribution.

Food The sea nettle feeds on small marine creatures and plankton. It captures food with the aid of nematocysts on its tentacles and oral arms. The moon jelly feeds mostly on plankton which catch on the sticky undersurface of the main part of its body as it moves through the water in a series of up and down motions. The oral arms then reach up to scrape off the plankton and carry it to the mouth which is located at the base of the arms.

Life History Sperm or eggs develop within the body of both species and are then released into the water through the mouth. The moon jelly incubates its egg in a pouch on the oral arms. The egg develops into a free-swimming larva called a planula (plan-you-la) which looks much like a paramecium. After a few days of swimming about, the larva settles head first onto the ocean floor or on a rock outcrop and grows into a creature that resembles a many-armed hydra. It spends the winter growing and in late winter it begins to produce young saucer-shaped jellyfish stacked one on top of the other like meat patties. This hydra-like form, called a scyphistoma (sky-fi-stoe-ma), may live for several years, feeding and producing more young each winter. When the young have grown to a certain size, they break off the top of the stack and swim away. This stage is called an ephyra (e-fear-a). Moon jellyfish ephyra appear in the water just after spring thaw. Sea nettle ephyra appear in May or June. It takes 6 months or more for the ephyra to become adults. There is one generation per year.

Comments Jellyfish armed with stinging nematocysts make somewhat unpleasant and potentially dangerous swimming companions. Sea nettles can inflict painful stings on those they meet and in mid-summer they can drive swimmers from the water. One of the most deadly of the armed jellyfish is the Portuguese man-of-war which inhabits waters from the Gulf of Mexico to the West Indies. The Portuguese man-of-war is actually a colony of individuals held together by an air-filled bladder with a large crest on top. The bladder keeps the colony afloat and the crest, which stands above the water's surface, serves as a sail which can be set at an angle to the wind to move the colony through the water. Tentacles of the Portuguese man-of-war can be up to 30 m (98 ft) long and they stream out behind the colony fishing for prey. The venom in the nematocysts of this species is said to be almost as toxic as that of a cobra snake.

Color of jellyfish
The bell or umbrella of the sea nettle is translucent pink with 16 red bars running out from the centre. The tentacles and arms are milky white. The moon jelly is translucent white with pink insides (Note: because jellyfish are almost clear, they often reflect the color of the water around them).

Flatworm

Have you ever been slimed? Not many people have, except perhaps in their worst nightmares. However, down below the murky waters of our lakes and streams there are hundreds of small insects and crustaceans (krus-tay-shuns) being slimed every day. The creature that is the cause of this is not an alien from outer space. Rather it is a small flat slug-like animal called a freshwater planarian or flatworm.

During late summer the pond was filled with lush green plants and all kinds of aquatic animals such as hydras, protozoa, sponges, dragonfly larvae, water beetles, mosquito larvae, crustaceans, and minnows. Many of the creatures lived near the water's surface or amongst the plants. Others, however, preferred the cover of rocks and pebbles on the pond floor. One such creature was the flatworm. The flatworm was very skinny so it fit quite nicely into its home beneath a rock. From under the rock, the flatworm could detect would-be lunch prospects as they went by. Special cells in its body called chemoreceptors (key-moe-re-septers) also helped it find food. Sometimes the flatworm would venture out to search for dead or injured creatures that had fallen to the pond floor. On this particular day, the flatworm was heading out on just such a mission. The previous day it had been lucky enough to capture a hydra which it swallowed whole. The hydra was armed with a coating of nematocysts (barb-like arrows used to protect it from enemies), but the nematocysts did not hurt the flatworm. Instead, when the flatworm ate the hydra, the nematocysts moved through the flatworm's body to form a defensive layer in its own skin.

With a wave-like motion the well-armored little creature set out swirling through the water. It was not a good enough swimmer to capture fast-moving creatures, but it could corner its prey amongst the rocks. Since flatworms' eyes do not focus (they see only light), the flatworm's attack style was often more luck than anything else. Today luck was on its side; the first rock crevice it came to had a badly injured amphipod (am-fi-pod) under it (healthy amphipods are often too strong for the flatworm to catch). The amphipod was busy feeding on algae and did not see the flatworm until its bulky shadow blotted out the light. The amphipod tried to escape, but instead it became tangled in a gloppy layer of slime as the flatworm curled itself around its helpless victim. Then, using its long proboscis (pro-baw-sis) or mouth, which stuck out of the middle of its stomach, the flatworm pumped the amphipod into the long branches of its stomach, which took the much needed food to various parts of the flatworm's body.

Soon it sensed that there was another flatworm close by. Sure enough, under a log not too far away, rested a second flatworm. The two worms swirled around each other, mated, and then both went their separate ways to lay eggs, since all flatworms are both male and female. One flatworm chose a flattened rock in a deeper part of the pond and laid several groups of two to three eggs on a stalk-like cocoon. Now it had provided a new generation of flatworms for the next year.

Phylum Platyhelminthes

Class Turbellaria

Size Flatworms range greatly in size. Some are so tiny they are able to live between the sand grains in tidal areas, while others grow to over 30 cm (12 in) in length. The flatworm in the story is called a freshwater planarian. It is approximately 5 mm (.2 in) long.

Distribution There are over 3,000 species of flatworms worldwide. Some live in oceans, a few live on land, while others such as the freshwater planarian live in lakes, streams, and ponds.

Food Although many parasitic species exist, flatworms are mainly scavengers and carnivores feeding mostly on dead animal material, some small invertebrates such as water fleas, copepods, and amphipods, and some fish eggs. Flatworms handle food by wrapping themselves around it, entangling it in slime, and pinning it to the ground. They then use their tube-like mouths, which are located in the middle of the underside of their bodies, to suck or pump their prey in. Food is transported to the rest of the body via a sac or series of folded tubes which branch out along the length of the body.

Life History Flatworms have two methods of reproducing. They can split in half and re-grow or regenerate the missing end, or they can reproduce sexually. Every flatworm has both male and female parts. This does not mean that a flatworm can mate with itself, but each worm can produce eggs. There are two types of eggs produced: summer eggs (with thin shells) and thick-shelled winter eggs.

In freshwater lakes of temperate regions, reproduction during the summer is mainly by regeneration. In the spring or early summer, the freshwater planarians may also mate and produce egg cases, each containing several eggs as well as nutritive yolk cells. These brownish-colored capsules are often found glued by a long stalk to rocks and other debris. Development takes 2 to 3 weeks after which the young flatworms hatch and swim away. There may be several generations per season. Most species overwinter as adults.

Comments Notice that the flatworms look as if they are cross-eyed. This is because the dark pigment is located to one side of the eye. The position and shape of the pigment cup allows light to enter only from one side of either eye. So although flatworms cannot focus on objects, they can tell direction and intensity of light and can see movement and shadows.

Color of flatworm
Flatworms are reddish-brown with gray edges. The amphipod is greenish-white.

Tapeworm

It was a lovely day for a walk. Andy and his dog Baker were enjoying a romp through the field when suddenly the young retriever found the trail of something interesting.

"Baker! Leave that dead rabbit alone!" cried Andy. "Ugh, wait 'til Mom and Dad see you." Andy took Baker by the collar and led him off towards home. Later, after Andy had washed Baker off, he told his parents of their adventure.

"Sounds like Baker found a fresh kill," said Andy's dad. "Probably coyotes."

"Did you say Baker ate some of the rabbit?" asked Andy's mother. Andy nodded. He wished he had run faster.

"I suppose a bit of raw meat won't hurt him," said his father. "But Dr. Wilson always warns us about letting the dogs eat raw meat."

A few weeks later, however, Andy noticed that Baker was not quite as lively as usual. Andy's dad was taking one of the cows to see Dr. Wilson, so they decided to take Baker too.

"Hmmm," Dr. Wilson said. "Has Baker been eating any raw meat lately?"

"Well, there was that dead rabbit a while back," said Andy's dad.

"This is a tapeworm," said Dr. Wilson as he held up a jar with a long flat worm-like thing floating in it. "It lives in the small intestines of meat-eating animals. Dogs get tapeworms from eating raw meat infected with immature tapeworms or from accidentally eating infected fleas."

Dr. Wilson put on rubber gloves and took something off Baker's tail. He went to his microscope and motioned for Andy to follow. Through the lense Andy could see a rice-like object.

"That is an egg-filled body segment of a tapeworm," explained Dr. Wilson. "There are many kinds of tapeworms, most of which spend their adult life in the intestines of meat-eating mammals such as dogs, cats, coyotes, and even humans. They attach the front end of their bodies to the wall of the animals' intestines and gradually grow longer and longer as they feed on partially digested food. Once the tapeworm reaches a certain age, it produces eggs in the oldest segments of its body. These segments are then released in the animal's feces. The eggs stay dormant or at rest on the ground until some plant-eating animal accidentally eats them. The eggs hatch inside this animal's body and the resulting larva, called a bladderworm, burrows through the intestine wall, enters the bloodstream, and travels to muscle tissue in another part of the animal's body where it then burrows in and forms a cyst. The cyst develops into a tapeworm when a meat-eating animal, like Baker here, eats the plant-eating animal."

"How do we get rid of the tapeworm now?" asked Andy.

"This medication will do the trick," answered Dr. Wilson. "But there may be eggs around your house and property that must be removed.

"We'll be sure to wash Baker's bed, vacuum the rec-room, and Andy, it will be your job to clean the yard," said Andy's dad. Andy nodded.

"You also should check Baker for fleas," advised Dr. Wilson. "Fleas can also give dogs tapeworms."

Phylum Platyhelminthes

Class Cestoidea

Size Adult tapeworms of some species can reach up to 12 m (40 ft) in length. A mature tapeworm of the species in this story is usually 60 cm to 2 m (24 in to 6.4 ft) long and 5 mm (.2 in) in width. The intermediate bladderworm stage may reach 10 cm (4 in) in length.

Distribution Tapeworms can be found all over the world. The tapeworms discussed in this story are common throughout North America.

Food Tapeworms feed on the contents of their host's digestive tract (a host is an animal that has another creature feeding on or in it). Tapeworms have no digestive tract; food is simply absorbed through the outer membrane or skin of the body.

Life History Adult tapeworms live in the intestines of meat-eating mammals including dogs, cats, and humans. When the tapeworm reaches maturity, it releases, one by one, its end body segments into the intestine to be passed in the feces. Each of these body segments contains many eggs. Once on the ground, the eggs can be accidentally eaten by an intermediate host, an animal that supports the life of an immature or intermediate life stage of the parasite. This animal could be a flea, mite, fish, cow, pig, horse, elk, deer, rabbit, rodent, or even a human (the intermediate hosts of the tapeworm in this story are rabbits, hares, rarely rodents). Different species of tapeworms have different intermediate hosts. Once the egg is in the intestine of one of these animals, it hatches and the resulting larva, called a bladderworm, burrows through the intestinal wall and enters the bloodstream. From there it often ends up in the animal's muscles where it forms a bladder-like cyst which will become active again only after its host is eaten by a meat-eating mammal or carnivore. If this happens, the cyst will attach itself by means of suckers or hooks, to the wall of the intestine of its new host. It will then develop into an egg-laying adult.

Comments There are a number of different species of tapeworms in North America. In most, the adult stage develops in carnivorous mammals. The intermediate hosts, however, vary greatly. There are at least 12 species that can infect dogs, 7 that infect cats, and 3 that infect humans. The species most commonly infecting dogs has its intermediate stage in a flea. Another species of tapeworm has 2 intermediate stages: one in crustaceans, the other in fish. People are susceptible to tapeworms when they eat partially raw meat. It is a good rule never to handle the feces of any meat-eating animal, to always wash plants before eating them, and never to eat very rare meat.

Color of tapeworm
The tapeworm is yellowish-white; its surroundings, an animal's small intestine, can be shades of pink and red. The bladderworm is also yellowish-white.

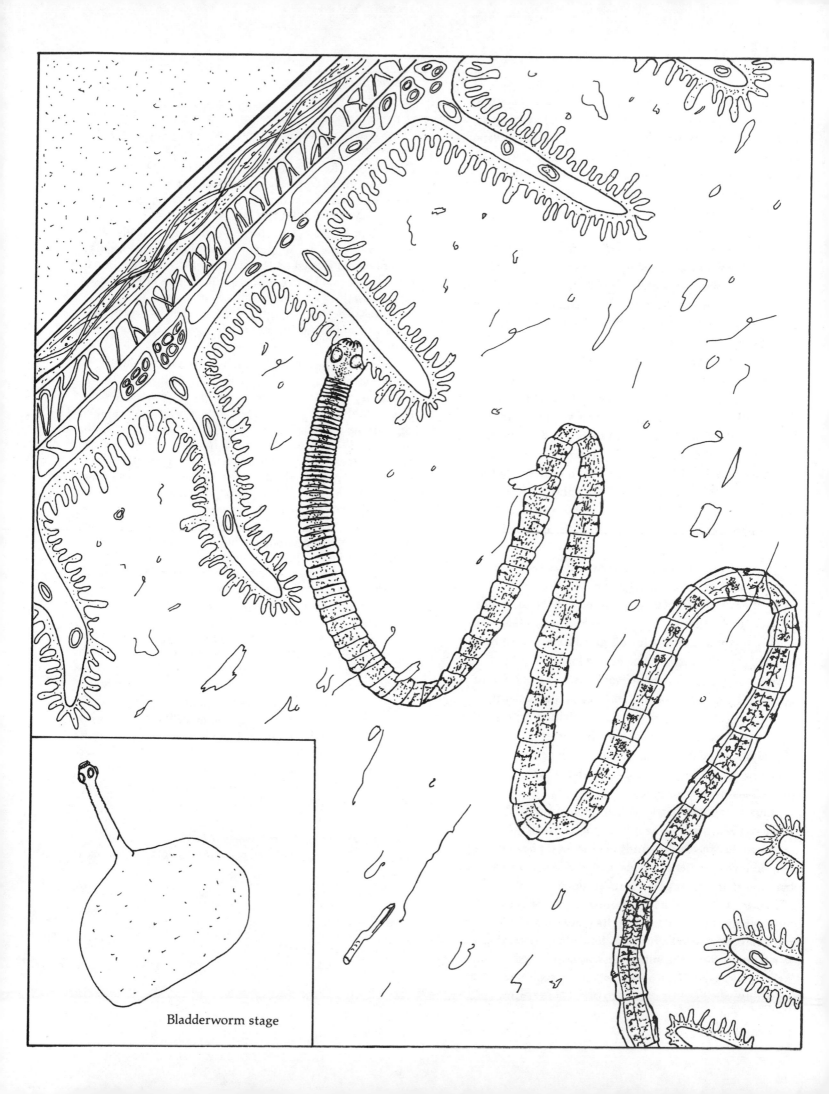

Bladderworm stage

Rotifer

It was amazing! Chris had never seen anything like it. The world beneath her microscope was totally new and strange. As an introduction to using the microscope, her teacher, Mr. Rochon, had given each student a drop of pond water to examine. Mr. Rochon had explained that they would see many different creatures and plants in the pond water. There would be long chains of plant cells called algae, tiny beautifully shaped plants called diatoms (die-a-toms), and one-celled animals called protozoa which swim about using whip-like tails or flagella. There was even one protozoan called an amoeba that moved by sloshing body fluid from one part of its body to another. But the neatest creature of all was the rotifer. The rotifer, Mr. Rochon had told them, was one of the smallest multi-celled creatures in the world. Rotifers come in many shapes and sizes. Some live in colonies secured to a rock or the pond floor, while others live alone, securing themselves to a plant or rock by a long stalk.

Chris liked the ones that swam about freely the best. Her teacher had explained that these rotifers moved either by creeping leech-style using glue in their tiny feet to grip the surface as the head end stretched forward, or by swimming, using two propeller-like circles of cilia on the top of their heads. These circles of cilia called trochal (tro-cal) discs beat in a circular motion, making a current that could propel them through the water or help them draw in and capture food. Chris giggled as she imagined tiny helicopters floating about in the pond water. As tiny as they were, the rotifers even had a digestive system. Mr. Rochon had shown them a picture. He had pointed out the black dots that were the rotifer's simple eyes, and the two teeth-like bands in its mouth that helped it grind food. It also had a stomach, small intestines, and even a bladder.

Chris really hoped that she would be lucky enough to have a rotifer in her drop of pond water. She patiently moved the dish around, all the time watching through the lens. There were many algae and a few protozoa. Chris stopped her searching for a moment so she could draw one of the protozoa. Then suddenly a rotifer wheeled into sight. Chris was very excited.

"I found one!" she exclaimed. "I found a rotifer."

One of her friends came over to look. "Neat!" she exclaimed. "I can see the bands of cilia on its head move. They do look like little wheels, and look, you can see little plant pieces and stuff going into its mouth!"

Chris looked into the lens. Sure enough the rotifer was drawing tiny food particles into its mouth. Even a nearby protozoan seemed to be having a hard time swimming away from it. Soon the entire class was clustered around Chris's desk, even Mr. Rochon. What a special discovery this had been.

Phylum Rotifera

Class Bdelloidea

Size Rotifers range in size from .04 mm (.002 in) to 3 mm (.1 in). They are one of the smallest multi-celled creatures in the world.

Distribution Rotifers are found throughout the world. Although their favorite habitat is freshwater, some species live in saltwater and a few live in mosses. There are approximately 1,500 known species worldwide.

Food The rotifer in this story is a suspension feeder. Tiny plant and animal particles are drawn to the mouth in the water current caused by the beating of the cilia surrounding the rotifer's mouth. Some species of rotifers are predators feeding on protozoa, other rotifers, and small aquatic creatures. They capture prey with tweezer-like teeth which project from the mouth or buccal cavity to seize their victims.

Life History The life stage in which rotifers spend the winter depends on where they live. Those living in temporary ponds and streams that dry up in late fall or freeze right to the ground, spend the winter as thick-shelled eggs. In the spring, the dormant eggs hatch and the rotifers that emerge from the eggs are all females. These produce eggs which give rise to more females, each having a life span of 1 or 2 weeks. Later in the season, as day length and food decrease, many rotifers produce eggs that provide both male and female individuals. Overwintering eggs are produced by this generation. In species living in permanent bodies of water there may or may not be overwintering eggs. The population may instead go through a series of peaks and cycles. Species that belong to the class Bdelloidea, including the one in this story, do not produce males at all. When winter approaches or when dry conditions exist, the bdelloids do not produce eggs. Instead, they secrete a gelatinous cover around themselves which hardens to form a protective cyst. Within this cyst the rotifer can withstand extreme cold and dry conditions for up to 50 years. In most species of rotifers there are several generations per year.

Comments The name "rotifer" originated as a description of how the body part that helps many of the members of this group move from one place to another. A crown of hair or cilia located on the rotifer's head end beats in a circular wave, propelling the animal through the water. Some species in this group move with a leech-like motion while a few others do not move at all.

Color of rotifer
The body of the rotifer is transparent (you can see through it), but may be green, orange, red, or brown, depending on what it has been eating.

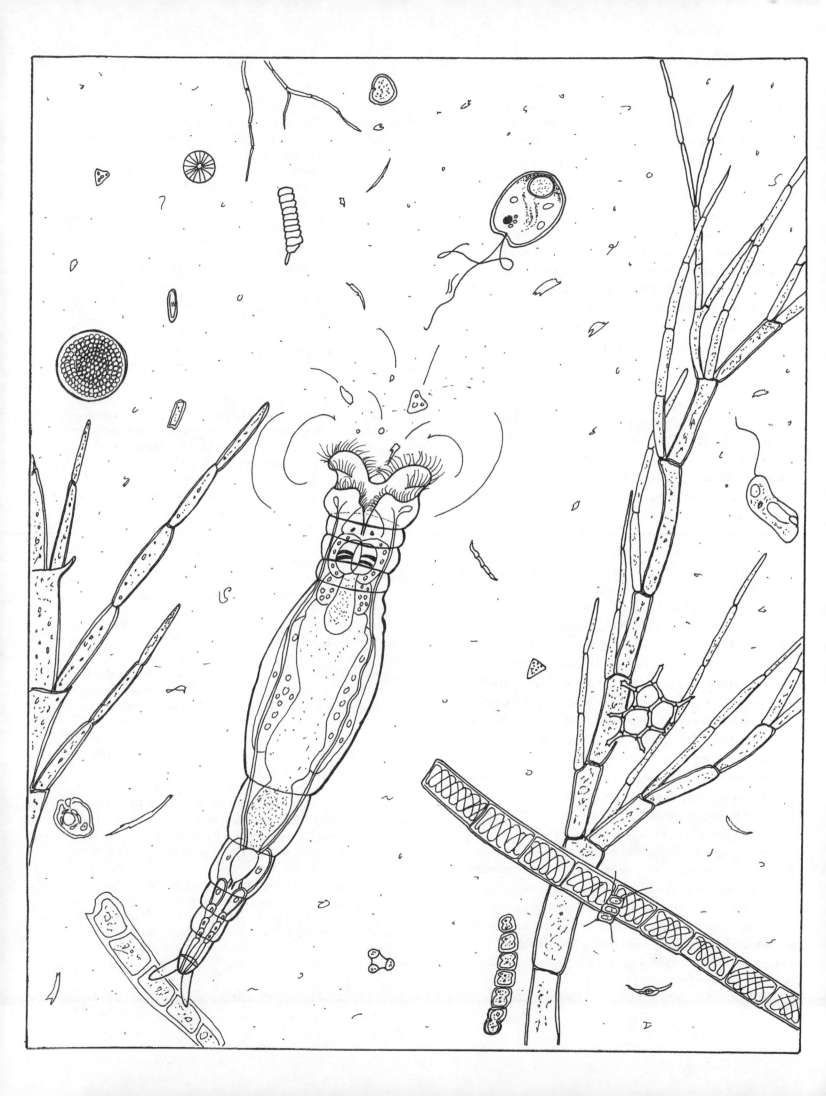

Nematode

Cory was so disappointed. Of all the fascinating creatures in the invertebrate world, she had been given one of the most disgusting to do a project on. Nematodes. Ugh!

Cory entered the reference library and the librarian helped her find some books on nematodes. Cory soon discovered some interesting facts. There are thousands of different species of these worm-like animals and each species feeds on specific types of food. She read about one that lives in muscle tissue of mammals, including people. This nematode can cause much damage and swelling. There was a photograph of a boy with a horribly swollen leg. She learned that the condition is called elephantiasis (elephan-tie-a-sis) and is caused by a nematode that lives only in tropical countries. She discovered that pinworms and roundworms (often found in dogs) are both nematodes. She also read about a nematode that hitches rides on the legs of insects in order to get from one lump of manure (which they eat) to another.

Finally Cory read about some nematodes that she felt she could write about without getting queasy. These nematodes live in the soil. Some feed on plant rootlets and dead plant material; others feed on the mud itself. Cory learned that rich soil contains millions of nematodes, and while these animals are often microscopic (not visible to the eye), they are very important for the soil.

Cory wrote down as much information as she could and then chose one book to take home with her. The book had instructions on how to capture soil nematodes. When Cory got home at lunch-time, she borrowed one of her mother's funnels, some cheesecloth, and a drinking glass. Then she dug some of the rich soil out of their garden, placed it in the glass, and folded the cheesecloth several times over the top of the glass. An elastic band kept the cheesecloth in place as she carried her treasure to school. In class, her teacher let her set up the experiment. She sealed the end of the funnel and filled it with water. Then she turned the glass upside down to rest on top of the funnel.

"The book said that nematodes will crawl through the cheesecloth to get to the water in the funnel," she explained to her classmates.

Sure enough, the next day, when they placed a drop of the water on a microscope slide, Cory and her classmates discovered hundreds of tiny nematodes squirming about. Cory explained how the nematodes move by twisting through the soil. She also explained how many nematodes get through unpleasant conditions by pumping the water out of their bodies until they become "dry powder" which is often used as fish food. The nematodes "come back to life" when water is added.

Phylum   Nematoda

Class   Secernentea (Phasmida)

Size   Most freshwater and land-dwelling nematodes are less than 1 mm (.04 in) in length. However, some marine species can grow as long as 50 mm (2 in). The parasitic New Guinea thread worm, which attacks connective tissue of mammals, is only 1 mm (.04 in) thick, but can grow as long as 120 cm (47 in). The largest known nematode species is found in the placenta of sperm whales and can be up to 9 m (30 ft) long!

Distribution   With over 100,000 species in the world, nematodes can be found from the polar regions to the tropics in all types of environments — deserts, mountains, hot springs, oceans. The nematodes in this story can be found in rich moist humus soil of forests all over North America.

Food   The diet varies with the species and can include other small creatures, plant material, dead plant and animal material, animal droppings, bacteria, fungi, and even mud. There are also many species that are parasites, that is, they feed on or in living things including mammals. The species in this story feed on plants, bacteria, other small creatures, and organic material in the soil. When feeding, plant parasite nematodes like the three pictured in the drawing, use a stylet (sti-let), a needle-like spear, to pierce into the plant and suck out the juices. Some predatory nematodes also have a stylet which they use to spear other nematodes. In other nematodes, food is captured by grasping it with a series of jaw-like teeth or one blade-like tooth. The food is then either swallowed whole or the juices are sucked out (depending on the species and the food item).

Life History   Soil nematodes use three types of reproduction. The most common method involves both a female and a male nematode. After mating and fertilization, some females lay thick-shelled eggs, while others give birth to live young. The eggs can withstand the cold temperatures of winter. In the second type of reproduction, the individual worms are hermaphroditic (herm-afro-dit-ick), that is, each worm has both male and female organs. Sperm is produced first and then stored until the eggs develop. Once the eggs are mature, the sperm is released from storage to fertilize the eggs still within the worm's body. The fertilized eggs are then laid in the soil. The third type of reproduction is called parthenogenesis (par-thin-o-gen-e-sis) where female nematodes give birth to more female nematodes without being fertilized by a male. For some free-living soil nematodes, from egg to adult takes less than 3 days; the total life span is 30 days for females and 25 days for males.

Comments   So common are the nematodes that .4 ha (1 acre) of good farm soil can contain several hundred million to over a billion nematodes. One decomposing apple on the ground of an orchard can have over 90,000 nematodes in it! Some of our most serious parasite enemies are in the nematode phylum.

Color of nematode
Nematodes are off-white. The soil and wood particles can be brown, black, beige, and green. Spaces around the nematodes are bluish (the water layer that often connects them with nearby soil particles).

Earthworm

A bright flash lit up the dark forest clearing as rain began to patter everywhere. The earth greedily soaked up the moisture. Soon small puddles began to appear and run-off water seeped into small holes and tunnels made by forest animals. A small earthworm in its burrow shrugged a droplet of water off its body. Nighttime is a busy time for earthworms as they search for little tidbits of rotting plant or animal material. This sudden downpour did not help at all. In fact, if the rain did not lighten soon, the earthworm would have to leave its burrow or drown. Although the skin of earthworms must always be moist because they breath through their skin, too much water can cut off the oxygen supply and they could suffocate.

The rain continued and the earthworm made its way to the surface. Wiggle, wiggle. Tiny bands of muscle along its body length and small barbs or bristles on its skin helped the earthworm cling to and climb up the damp walls of its burrow. The open ground of the forest floor was a dangerous place to be. There were many enemies that would enjoy a tasty earthworm meal, so the earthworm had to be very alert to any vibrations that might signal another animal's approach. All five of the earthworm's tiny hearts beat hard as it wiggled around a large puddle near the burrow entrance. The earthworm stopped a moment to gulp down a small piece of leaf and some earth.

The earthworm did not wander far from its burrow, for morning would come soon and the harsh drying rays of the sun would kill it very quickly. It collected pieces of food that it would eat later in the safety of its burrow. When the rain stopped, the worm wiggled back towards its burrow. Light-sensing organs on its skin told the earthworm that the sun was rising and soon worm-loving birds would be on the prowl. The worm quickly dragged itself and its collection of food into its burrow. Suddenly, a terrible thumping vibrated through the soil. "Thump, thump, thump, poke!" It was a robin and it was peering into the earthworm's hole. The worm squirmed farther down the burrow just in time to miss the sharp point of the robin's beak! "Poke, poke." The robin tried again. Then suddenly, the robin spotted the tail end of a neighboring earthworm that had been a bit slower in returning to its burrow. "Thump, thump, thump." The robin hopped over, reached into that worm's burrow, and after a short tug of war, gobbled it up. Then an insect caught its attention and the robin hopped off in another direction.

What a close call! The danger was gone, but the earthworm would have to be more cautious if it was to live to its tenth birthday.

Phylum   Annelida

Class   Oligochaeta

Size   Earthworms range in size from a few mm (a fraction of an inch) to 3.6 m (12 ft) in length (the giant Australian earthworm). The earthworm in this story averages 13 to 15 cm (5 to 6 in) in length when mature.

Distribution   Earthworms can be found in rich damp soil throughout the world.

Food   Earthworms eat all kinds of organic material including decaying vegetables, leaves, bits of root, grass cuttings, and dead or decaying animals and insects. They actually have taste buds and prefer certain types of food over others. Earthworms pull pieces of food into their burrows and swallow the food mixed with soil. They have no teeth so they use soil particles to help grind the food. Grinding is done in a muscular section of the worm's throat which is called the gizzard. Earthworms are very important in the cycling and mixing of soil nutrients and actually improve plant growth.

Life History   In spring when the soil warms up, the earthworms' mating season begins. Earthworms are hermaphrodites, each worm having both male and female organs. Most earthworms however, still must mate with another worm in order to produce young. Some worms travel a long way to find a mate, while others mate on the earth's surface with the worm in the next burrow while keeping their tail ends safely anchored in their own tunnels during the whole process. After mating, a band of mucus is secreted by the swollen ring or band of skin called a clitellum (kly-tell-um) near the worm's head. The band of mucus slides forward over the body of the worm. As it passes over the reproductive organs it picks up a number of eggs (usually 4 or 5, but sometimes as many as 20) and some sperm that was deposited in a special pocket on its body by another worm. The eggs are then fertilized and the band slides off the worm's head. Both ends of the band seal to form a little yellow capsule. The baby worms hatch 14 to 21 days later. The 1 to 2 cm (.5 to 1 in) long babies will take 90 days to mature and can live to be 10 to 12 years of age in captivity (in the wild, they probably live only a year or two). There is more than one generation per year.

Comments   Earthworms keep their bodies moist by coating themselves in a sticky liquid called mucus which is secreted by glands in the skin. The skin must be moist at all times because earthworms have no lungs — they breathe through their skins! Oxygen dissolves in mucus and then passes into the body and the bloodstream.

In some parts of the country, raising earthworms is big business. Earthworms are very important to farmers. They are good fertilizers of the soil, plus they are a favored live bait for fishing. In some resorts you can find vending machines that sell cartons of 20 worms for a dollar.

Color of earthworm
Earthworms are pinkish-yellow. The robin should be gray-brown with a rusty red breast.

Leech

The leech was hungry. It preferred cattle or human blood, but frog eggs and tadpoles could also provide a tasty meal. As a young leech, it had eaten insect larvae and worms, but these creatures no longer seemed satisfying now that the leech was an adult.

Just then the leech noticed two pairs of dark shadows near the water surface. It contracted the muscles on the sides of its body until it was as long and flat as it could be. Stretching towards the shadows, it could feel vibrations in the water. With a graceful waving motion it set off to investigate. As it came close, the tastebud-like sensors on the sides of its body sensed an unmistakable flavor in the water. Human feet! The leech excitedly moved in for a scrumptious blood meal.

"Look out Doug!" warned Joey. "There's a leech coming towards your feet." Doug quickly lifted his feet only to bang them on the side of the dock.

"Ouch!" he grunted. "You've got leeches in your pond?"

"All kinds of them," said Joey as the two boys peered down into the murky water. The leech was still swimming about, trying to find its lost meal. The light sensors on its head told it that there were shadows above but the smell was gone. Joey reached down with his dip net and scooped up the leech. As he plopped it into his pail the leech contracted its body muscles, becoming as small as possible.

"Ugh, don't touch it," shouted Doug as Joey picked the leech up in his fingers. "It's going to stick to you!" Doug could just imagine the blood oozing out of his friend's fingers.

"Look, it has a sucker at either end of its body," explained Joey. "It uses the suckers to hold onto plants and stuff, and to move, inchworm-style. The front sucker is its mouth. Inside its mouth there are three long blades which it uses to cut open your skin once it's attached. It can take up to twenty milliliters (one ounce) of blood in one meal!"

"Impossible!" exclaimed Doug. "It's too small to swallow that much blood."

"Well that's what my mom told me," said Joey. "She said that leeches have fast-working organs that can take a lot of the water out of blood, leaving only the good stuff to be digested. Once their stomachs are full, they drop off your skin to finish digesting the meal in safety."

Just then, a huge brightly colored leech swam by. Its size made it look more like a snake than a leech.

"Wow!" exclaimed Doug as he backed away from the edge of the dock. "Look at the size of that one! I'm glad we're not swimming in there. Imagine how much blood it would suck out of you!" Doug shivered at the thought.

That's a horse leech," said Joey. "It preys on insects, worms, and snails. Rarely will it eat mammal blood."

"No!" said Doug. He had never heard of leeches that didn't suck blood.

"It's true!" said Joey. "Not all leeches are parasites, and many are scavengers. There are some that attack turtles, frogs, and salamanders. Others only attack fish. In our part of the country, only one species of leech eats human blood."

Phylum Annelida

Class Hirudinea

Size Leeches vary in size from 1 to 30 cm (.5 to 12 in) depending on the species. The average length is 2 to 5 cm (1 to 2 in). The horse leech is approximately 20 cm (8 in); the American medicinal leech is 4 to 12 cm (1.5 to 5 in).

Distribution Although leeches are found throughout the world, living on land, in saltwater, and freshwater, they are most common in northern temperate freshwater lakes and ponds.

Food Several species of leeches are blood sucking ectoparasites (ek-toe-para-sites) that feed on the outside of other living creatures (often without killing them). Some leeches feed on fish, some on frogs, turtles, and snails. The American medicinal leech prefers to feed on mammals, but it may also eat frogs' eggs, worms, and insect larvae. Other species, such as the horse leech, are predators attacking invertebrates such as snails, crustaceans, and insects (only rarely will it attack mammals). In its search for food, the horse leech can leave the water to wander on shore feeding on earthworms which they swallow whole. Leeches hang onto their prey with the help of a large sucker that surrounds the mouth. The blood-sucking species use 3 blade-like jaws to cut their victim's flesh. They then fill the wound with saliva containing chemicals which make the skin go numb (so you can't feel the leech bite), and a chemical called hirudin (hi-rude-in). Hirudin stops blood from clotting, making it easier for the leech to feed. Fish-attacking species actually force their whole mouth into the victim's tissues.

Life History Like earthworms, leeches are hermaphrodites, each leech has both male and female body parts. Mating occurs in spring to early autumn. The eggs, which are laid anywhere from 2 days to many months after mating, are enclosed in a cocoon which protects them from drying and freezing and contains a nourishing fluid. The cocoon holds one or several eggs depending on the species. Each leech produces several cocoons each year. The cocoons are attached to rocks and underwater plants, or are buried in damp soil outside the pond. A few species carry their young around with them.

Comments Blood sucking leeches can take in 10 times their own weight in blood.

Color of leech
The medicinal leech (the smaller one) is dark green or black with red and black spots on its back and bright reddish-orange underneath. The horse leech is blotchy gray-green with a red line on the edge of its back. There is an orange-red stripe on its belly.

Snail and Mussel

Margaret, the park naturalist, was doing her rounds of the park lakeshore trail. As she began her walk on the sandy shore, she met a small boy who smiled shyly at her.

"See the shell I found?" he said as he held out a large brown snail shell. "I found it near the marsh."

"Hey, that's great!" said Margaret in an encouraging tone.

"How do all the snail's body parts fit in such a small shell?" he asked.

"Well," said Margaret, "some snails actually don't fit in their shells, and many ocean-living snails don't have any shells at all when they first hatch! They swim freely for the first part of their lives, slowly developing a shell as they grow. The shell you are holding belonged to a freshwater giant pond snail. Pond snails look just like tiny adult snails when they hatch. But while they are in their eggs they go through some amazing changes. At first they look very simple like paramecium. Then their body parts start to form. As they develop, the portion of the body that contains the vital organs slowly begins to twist so that the nerve cord twists, the heart loops, and the gills, anus, and the space surrounding them eventually end up facing the snail's head instead of the back of the body. After that, the shell starts to grow, fitting the shape of the body. By the time the snail hatches, everything is balanced. There is space for a lung, and all body openings face outward," she explained.

"That sounds pretty complicated," said the boy.

"Not if you are a snail I suppose," laughed Margaret.

"Look! A clam shell," exclaimed the boy as he ran ahead to pick up a large brown and gold mussel shell. "Why do clams have two shells?"

"Many clams or mussels like to dig in mud and sand," said Margaret. "The smooth, flattened shape of their shell makes digging easier and cleaner too."

"Pretty gritty," laughed the boy. "You know, they must lead a real boring life, living in the mud like that."

"Actually their lives are quite interesting," said Margaret. "Mother mussels of this species protect their eggs until they hatch. They may lay up to three million eggs. The young, called clappers, which move by clapping their shells open and shut, leave the mother soon after hatching and must "clap" onto a passing fish if they can! Once attached to the fish, the clappers make the fish form a growth or cyst that covers the clams and protects them as they feed on the fish. After a few weeks the clappers develop into young adults, break out of their cysts, and settle to the bottom to burrow in. Mussels use their foot to dig into the sand. Once the foot is in far enough, the end of the foot widens to form an anchor. They then pull themselves down into the sand until only the two siphon openings are above the sand."

"That's wild!" exclaimed the boy. Just then they saw his parents coming up the trail. "Wait 'til my parents hear about this."

Phylum Mollusca

Class Gastropoda (snails and slugs) *Class* Bivalva (oysters, clams, mussels, and scallops)

Size The giant pond snail averages 4.5 cm (1.75 in) in length. The freshwater mussel can grow as long as 15 cm (6 in).

Distribution Both species are found throughout Canada and northern United States. The pond snail lives in freshwater lakes, ponds, and marshes. The freshwater mussel is common in lakes, rivers, and streams.

Food The pond snail uses its file-like tongue or radula to scrape algae off rocks, logs, and plants beneath the water's surface. Mussels eat microscopic plant and animal material. They do not have a radula; instead they create a current to draw water and food particles into their bodies through a siphon by the beating of hundreds of tiny hairs or cilia located within their gills. The food particles are trapped on a net-like mucous strip which covers the gills. Large particles are drawn along a food groove between the gills and into the mouth. There, food is wound into a ball of mucous and further sorted within the stomach. Waste materials are flushed out along with water that is leaving the body.

Life History Freshwater snail Unlike saltwater species, pond snails hatch as miniature adults (saltwater forms have a free-swimming larval stage). Each snail has both male and female parts and after self-fertilizing or exchanging sperm with one another, each snail lays one hundred or more eggs enclosed in a clear jelly-like mass which is attached to plants or other objects in the water. The young snails emerge after 10 days. Snails overwinter in the adult stage.

Freshwater mussel Mussels have both male and female individuals. The males begin to release sperm into the water. The females take the sperm in along with incoming water and food particles. The female mussels brood their eggs between their gills. After hatching, the tiny larvae or clappers, as they are called, overwinter, leaving the mother the following spring. Equipped with tiny bivalve shells, the larvae sink to the bottom where they stay until a fish swims close enough for them to clap onto a fin or other body part (in some species the young stay within the mother until a fish swims by, and she ejects her young in the direction of the fish). The larva causes the fish's tissues to grow and surround it, forming a cyst. Within the cyst the larva lives and feeds for 10 to 30 days, gradually developing the organs of an adult mussel. The larva then breaks out of the cyst, falls to the bottom, and burrows into the mud or sand.

Comments There are over 20,000 species of bivalves. Some are burrowing filter feeders, others attach themselves by tiny strings to exposed rock. Some are predators while others are parasites or tunnel borers. A few have very well developed eyes on the tissue (mantle) all along the edge of the shells. Bivalves are important to us as food, in the production of pearls, and as garbage collectors because they filter harmful bacteria from the water.

Color of snail and mussel
The giant pond snail is light brown with a bluish-brown foot. The freshwater mussel is dark brown with light brown, gold, and black streaks. The mussel's foot is off-white.

Slug

Timmy was learning to scuba dive and brought along some underwater pictures he had taken to show his cousin Blanche.

"This is a nudibranch (nude-i-brank) or sea slug," he explained. "It's actually a snail that has no shell."

"Like the slugs that live in our garden?" said Blanche.

Timmy was not pleased with his cousin's comparison, but she was right. "Well, yes," he said, "but the sea slug is much more colorful and interesting. Sea slugs live in the ocean where they feed on hydra colonies, sea anemones, and other small animals. Plus," he continued, "they cover themselves in slime that is poisonous or tastes terrible to their enemies. Their bright orange and blue colors actually warn enemies to stay away."

"Hmmm," said Blanche. "The slugs in our garden are covered in slime too, but I think their slime is to help them move and to prevent them from drying out." Blanche looked at the picture again, "What are all those funny finger-like things on its back?" she asked.

"In some sea slugs those are lungs. This one uses only the nobs (called cerata) at the back of its body as lungs. The others contain poisonous darts that the animal absorbs from the body of its prey. If an enemy tries to touch or bite one of the nobs, it ends up with a mouthful of stinging darts."

The next day when Timmy arrived, Blanche handed him a small plastic container. Inside was a pinkish-gray garden slug.

"Is this what you wanted to show me?" giggled Timmy.

"It's a garden slug," she answered in a serious tone. "Did you know that land slugs and snails breathe through a lung? They also have a heart, a stomach, a liver, and a kidney. They even have a nervous system that forms a ring around the heart and has branches running throughout the body."

Before Timmy could interrupt, Blanche continued with her little lesson.

"Snails and slugs have a mouth on the foot," she giggled, "the tongues are covered in tiny teeth which scrape food into the mouth as they lick the surface they're walking on."

Timmy opened his mouth to speak but Blanche cut him off.

"Look at its tentacles. There are four of them. Did you know that snails have eyes on the ends of one set of tentacles and use the other smaller set to smell with?"

By this time Blanche was totally out of breath and her cousin was totally impressed (although he would never let her know that).

"Well, that's all very interesting," he responded. "But our land slugs and sea slugs are still bigger and more colorful than yours. When you come to visit us, I'll show you," he bragged.

Blanche just smiled. She knew she had outdone her cousin this time — no matter what he said.

Phylum   Mollusca

Class   Gastropoda

Size   The gray garden slug is 25 to 35 mm (1 to 1.5 in) in length; the nudibranch is 83 mm (2.3 in) long.

Distribution   There are over 35 species of land slug in North America. The common garden slug is found in moist vegetated areas throughout the continent. The nudibranch is found on rocky shores, bays, and estuaries along the west coast from Alaska to Baja California.

Feeding   The gray garden slug feeds on fresh plant material. The opalescent nudibranch feeds on hydroids and other invertebrates — even other nudibranchs. In each the mouth opens into a cavity with a rasping tongue or radula. Food is taken in with a licking or scraping motion. Saliva glands secrete a mucous which lubricates the radula and entangles the food item. The whole mass is then swallowed.

Life History   *Land slugs*   All individuals can lay eggs. Mating is usually preceded by a courtship involving circling plus tentacle and body contact. After mating a small number of large yolky eggs are laid in damp leaf litter or some other sheltered location. After 3 to 4 weeks the eggs hatch and the tiny whitish-colored young begin to feed. Three to 6 months later they reach full size. Although land slugs commonly overwinter in the egg stage, eggs may be laid throughout the summer.

Sea slugs   After exchanging sperm with its mate, the sea slug finds a safe place to lay its long spiral-shaped string of mucous-coated eggs. When the young slugs hatch, they have a snail-like shell. For the first 15 days they swim about freely with the aid of a special organ called a velum. The velum consists of two lobes covered in long movable hairs or cilia which propel the young through the water. The velum is also used to capture tiny food particles. The young slugs are referred to as veligers. When the veligers are 15 days old, they lose their velum and settle on some suitable surface to begin a crawling way of life. After a few more weeks they lose their shell and gradually the body flattens to take on the adult form.

Comments   Sea slugs are a very diverse, colorful, and indeed bizarre group of molluscs. Most species are carnivorous but there are a few plant eaters. One algae-eating species is known to store and gain energy from photosynthesizing chloroplasts taken from their algae prey. Sea slugs also come in many unusual shapes and colors. Some species have wing-like extensions on the foot which enable them to fly through the water with a flapping motion.

Most land slugs are not as colorful, but they can do much damage to gardens. A pan of stale beer placed in the garden will drown many slugs and is a popular remedy for slug overpopulation.

Color of slug

The garden slug is pinkish-gray with brown or gray blotches; the sea slug's body is bluish-white with a yellow and orange line down the middle of its back and sky-blue lines along its margins. The cerata (finger-like projections) are bright orange with white tips.

Giant Pacific Octopus

The young octopus (ok-toe-puss) crept along the ocean floor, cautiously reaching out one arm at a time. As he passed over a sandy spot, his skin changed color to blend in with his surroundings. He climbed over a large rock covered with anemones and scallops and carefully examined it with his eight long tentacle arms. It was important for him to find a crack or hole to call his own. All octopods have soft bodies, and many enemies including seals, sea otters, and even sharks, and various fishes find them very tasty.

Just then he noticed an old barrel half buried in the sand on the ocean floor. What a perfect home it would make. He quickly went to investigate, but it was not empty. Inside the barrel was a very large, grumpy mother octopus and her sixty thousand or so eggs. The rice-like eggs hung in strands from the ceiling of the barrel like hundreds of tiny white crystals in a long chandelier.

The mother octopus turned red with anger as she rushed out to meet the young intruder. Instinctively the young octopus knew that the mother octopus would fight to the death to protect her unhatched young, so he quickly backed away. He was no match for the meter- (3-ft-) long arms and sharp beak of the older, more experienced octopus. octopus.

Still feeling frightened, the octopus sucked in a big gulp of water and then spit it out through his siphon, sending him whirling through the water in a cloud of sand (called jet propulsion). With a second jet of water, he gracefully glided to the edge of the rocks. Would he be able to find a place to hide before an enemy found him?

He spread his arms out every which way, feeling here and there for an opening in the rock. He moved one arm downwards, and near the bottom the rock face ended, leaving a small space between it and the ocean floor. He explored the crevice with one of his arms and then grasped onto the underside of the rock and carefully pulled himself downward. The crack was small but octopods have no real bones so they are able to squeeze into amazingly tight spaces. Just then a seal came upon the octopus — in time to see the last two arms disappear under the rock. The seal grabbed hold of the tip of one of the arms and began to pull. The seal was strong but the octopus, with its hundreds of suction cups, was able to hold on firmly to the rock. Finally the seal gave up and left in search of an easier meal — its only reward for its efforts was a small piece of the octopod's arm.

After a few minutes the octopus relaxed, his skin changed from a frightened red/white to brown. He was missing the tip of one of his arms, but this would grow back. Now that danger was gone, he would begin to make his new home larger and more comfortable. Later, he would move out under cover of darkness to search for crabs and clams nearby, bringing them back to his den where he would feed on them at his leisure. Now he had found a home at last.

Phylum Mollusca

Class Cephalopoda (octopus, squid, cuttlefish, nautilus)

Size The giant Pacific octopus is the largest octopus species in the world. While the average is 2 m (6 ft) long (1.2 m or 4 ft of which are its arms or tentacles) and 14 to 19 kg (30 to 42 lbs), the largest giant Pacific octopus on record measured over 9 m (30 ft) and weighed 272 kg (600 lbs).

Distribution The giant Pacific octopus is found on rocky ocean shores in sub-tidal zones from Alaska to southern California and along the northwest Pacific coastline to the sea of Japan.

Food Crabs and clams are favorites, but the Pacific octopus also eats shrimp, scallops, abalones, various fish, and smaller octopods. The octopus searches for or pounces on any creature of suitable size that comes near, and uses its beak-like mouth to eat its catch. If the prey is a clam or other hard-shelled animal, the octopus will use its sharp beak to drill a hole in the shell and inject a venom which paralyzes the animal.

Life History The life of an octopus is relatively short — the species in this story lives only 3 to 4 years. Both males and females die soon after spawning. For the giant Pacific octopus, courtship and mating can take place anytime but egg laying often occurs from fall to spring. Approximately 40 days after mating, the female prepares her den for egg laying. She lays her eggs in long white strands and attaches them to the ceiling of the back of the den. The task takes several days and up to 100,000 eggs may be laid (average of 50,000). The female stays with the eggs for the entire incubation period of 4 months or more. During this time she will not eat and spends most of her time carefully cleaning and aerating the eggs and protecting them from intruders. By the time the eggs hatch, the mother octopus is very weak and she will soon die. Hatching takes place over several days. Once the 7 mm (.3 in) -long young leave the den, they are on their own and will spend 1 to 3 months feeding on plankton near the ocean surface. During this stage they are easy prey for hungry fish and other predators. Only 2 or 3 may survive to adults. When the young reach 50 mm (2 in) in length they head for rocky sheltered areas to choose a den or shelter of their own.

Comments Cephalopods are one of the most advanced groups in the invertebrate world. Octopods are able to solve problems too difficult for many higher vertebrates. Cephalopods have well developed eyes that are quite similar to our own. Their blood is bluish in color — not red like ours. In our blood the red color comes from iron in hemoglobin (he-moe-globe-in). The iron binds with oxygen and transports it to our cells. Cephalopods use hemocyanin (he-moe-sigh-a-nin), where copper (blue-green in color) is the oxygen carrier.

Color of octopus
Octopods change color according to their mood and surroundings (red when angry, white when very frightened). A resting octopus is usually reddish or brownish with fine black lines. The undersides of its arms are pinkish-brown. Its suckers and eyelids are white.

Woodtick

Louise and Angie were going out to groom the horses. It was early May and there were still a few puddles and mucky spots remaining from spring thaw. Louise pulled on her boots as Angie tied a second knot in her kerchief.

"Now remember to stay away from the oak trees," said Angie as they headed out the door.

Louise gave Angie a puzzled look. "Why do we have to stay away from oak trees? And why are you wearing a kerchief on your head on such a nice day?" asked Louise.

"It's woodtick season," replied Angie. "Woodticks live in oak trees and jump down onto your head as you walk under the trees."

"Angie, come with me, I want to show you something," said Louise.

Louise took her friend's hand and led her over to a large patch of grass. She then crouched down and began to examine the plants.

"What are you doing?" asked Angie.

"Look at this," said Louise. There on the tip of a young blade of grass was a woodtick, its front legs stretched out as if waiting to grab something. Louise gently blew a puff of air at the tick and it responded by excitedly waving its legs about.

"What is it doing down here in the grass and why is it waving its legs around like that?" blurted Angie.

"Many people think that ticks live in trees but they don't; its too dry for them up there. They live in grass where they can hide if it's hot and hunt when it's not. When they feel a shadow passing by or when they smell carbon dioxide from a mammal's breath, they stretch out their arms and try to grab onto the animal as it passes by. Once they are on your body, they look for a warm protected place like behind the knees, neck, or under your arms. Then they glue the mouth parts onto your skin and suck as much blood as they want before they drop off."

"Ugh, that sounds pretty gruesome," said Angie.

"It can be if you are a dog or a deer with many ticks on you," agreed Louise. "The females often take so much blood they become as big as dimes. They use the blood to develop eggs you know," she continued as she picked up one of the tiny creatures.

"Well," interrupted Angie, "since you know so much about the nasty creatures, you can help me get them off the horses."

"Oh, the horses!" said Louise. She had almost forgotten about them. "Yes, I've got some tweezers in my bag. I'll show you how to remove woodticks."

Angie rolled her eyes. Once her friend got started on a topic, it was hard to stop her.

Phylum Arthropoda

Class Arachnida

Size The adult American dog tick (woodtick) averages 5 mm (.2 in) in length.

Distribution The American dog tick (woodtick) is found in southern Canada east of Alberta and northern United States west to the Rockies. It lives in grasslands along the edge of wooded areas.

Food Both adults and young feed on the blood of mammals. Woodticks use glue-like saliva to firmly attach their mouthparts to the skin of their victims. Once attached, the woodtick penetrates the skin with its mouthparts and sucks the blood (ticks have a chemical in their saliva that stops the blood from clotting).

Life History In early spring adult woodticks emerge from winter hiding places in search of a blood meal. When air humidity is high (morning or evening) they climb to the tops of blades of grass where they cling with outstretched claws, waiting for a deer, dog, human, or other large mammal to walk by. Once on the host, the woodtick searches for a warm place to settle (nape of neck, underarms, buttocks). It then glues its mouthparts to the skin and begins to feed. The male will take about as much blood as a mosquito does, but the female takes as much blood as she can, often filling her abdomen to the size of a grape. When she can eat no more she drops to the ground in search of a sheltered spot in which to lay her eggs. The eggs are laid all in one batch, up to 3,000 of them. The female dies after laying the eggs. Two to 4 weeks later, tiny brown larvae begin to hatch. The larvae stay close together for the first few days — possibly to absorb more heat from the sun but more probably to attract mice and other small rodents. As the mice gobble up the tiny woodtick larvae, many of the ticks are able to clamber onto the mouse, and so the hunter becomes the victim. The larvae will feed on the mouse's blood until they literally no longer fit into their own skins. They then drop to the ground and shed their skin in a process known as molting. Once the new, larger skin has hardened, the tick, now called a nymph, will begin to search for a new host, usually another mouse or other rodent. By late summer or early fall the nymph is once again ready to shed its skin and prepare for the cold winter, which is spent hidden safely beneath the leaf litter (they may also overwinter in the larval stage). There is one generation per year.

Comments Woodticks belong to the same group as spiders and mites. They are different from insects in that the adults have 8 legs (adult insects have 6), and only 2 body parts — a head and abdomen (insects have 3 — head, thorax and abdomen).

Color of woodtick
The dog ticks (woodticks) are reddish-brown with a cream-white pattern on their backs.

Writing Spider

It was early morning and the air was fresh with the smell of newly fallen rain. The entire marsh, meadow, and everything in it looked fresh and alive — all except a little black and yellow writing spider. She was hard at work repairing the damage the rain storm had done to her web. The top half had been washed away and she would have to start again. Using her blade-like mouthparts called chelicerae (chell-i-sir-ay), she carefully cut the lines of her old web and ate as many threads as she could save. The silk would be digested and returned to the spider's silk glands. Then, standing on a tall grass stem, the spider let out a long line of silk from one of her spinnerets on the end of her abdomen.

A gentle breeze blew the silk thread onto grasses sixty centimeters (2 ft) away. Perfect! As the thread caught, the spider pulled it tight and then strengthened her new line with extra threads. She then walked out to the middle of the thread, attached a second thread and dropped down to the plants below. She attached the end of this second line to a sturdy plant and pulled the line tight. She now had a Y-shaped thread line as her scaffold. She then spun more lines, one this way, one that way — like the spokes of a bicycle wheel. Next, the round or spiral threads were added. These were the sticky threads that would be used to capture prey. The silk for these came from another of her spinnerets. Round and round she went. Finally, down the middle of the web, she made a comfortable zig-zag matt of silk on which to rest. After adding a few more support threads, the spider returned to the centre of her beautiful new web to wait for breakfast to arrive.

Sitting on the underside of the web, hidden from predators, the spider stretched out her slender legs so that the tip of each foot or tarsi was hooked onto a main thread of the web. Her tarsi were super sensitive to vibrations. That was important since writing spiders have very poor eyesight. Just then, the spider sensed a vibration coming from the thread under one of her front legs. She sat very still for a moment and then plucked the thread where she had felt the motion. Instantly the thread started to vibrate and from the motion and the strength of the vibration, the spider could tell how large the prey was and exactly where on the web to find it. In seconds the spider was on top of her prey. It was a large fly and it would easily escape if it was not trapped immediately. Using her back legs and silk from her spinnerets, the spider swiftly turned the poor fly over several times, securely wrapping it in silk. With a quick bite of venom from the spider's chelicerae, the fly became paralyzed. Then the spider carried her newly caught breakfast back to her resting spot in the middle of the web. Perhaps today would be a good day after all.

Phylum Arthropoda

Class Arachnida

Size Adult female writing spiders vary in length from 10 to 25 mm (.4 to 1 in). The male is much smaller: only 5 to 8 mm (.2 to .3 in) in length.

Distribution The writing spider makes its home on shrubs and herbs in marshy areas, or on grasses in gardens, meadows, and pastures throughout the United States and southeastern Canada.

Food The writing spider will attempt to capture and eat almost any insect that lands on its web. As soon as the spider senses prey on the web, it runs to it, fastens a sticky thread of silk to it, then using its back legs and a flow of silk, the spider rolls the prey over two or three times. Once the prey is securely wrapped, the spider paralyzes it with a quick bite of its chelicerae. Prey is eaten by pouring digestive juices into a wound made by the chelicerae. The spider then drinks the insect's digested body fluids.

Life History In late August and early September, the tiny male writing spider leaves his web in search of a mate. The female has a perfume called a pheromone (fair-eh-moan), which helps the male find her. Once he has found the web of a female, the male must make sure that the female does not think that he is something to eat. Carefully he sits at the edge of her web and gently plucks the silk strands in a special rhythm which only writing spiders recognize. After a short courtship, the male takes the sperm he has stored in special bulbs in his short leg-like pedipalps (ped-ee-palps), and transfers it to two special storage sacs on the female's abdomen. When the female is ready to lay her eggs, she chooses the top of a shrub or sturdy weed, creates a support of silk threads, and spins the upper half of the cocoon. The outside is dense silk, the inside is a finer mesh. She then lays her eggs up into the nest (about 100 of them), covers them with the sperm, and spins several more layers of protective silk on the bottom. The entire egg-sac is then covered in a parchment-like outside coating which seals the cocoon so that the eggs or young are protected from the cold winter winds. In spring, the young spiderlings hatch and eat their way out. They then climb to the tops of grass stems, spin long threads, and take a ride on the wind to a place to start their own webs. The life span is one year and there is one generation per year.

Comments Not all spiders spin webs. The funnel-web spiders build a silken funnel in which they hide. Trap door spiders live underground, waiting to ambush their prey from beneath a soil-covered trap door. Another species lives underwater.

Note: The venom of most spiders is not toxic to humans; however, black widow spiders, some of which are found in the United States and in southern Ontario and southern British Columbia have a nerve-damaging venom. The symptoms of a bite can be very painful. Fortunately, fatal cases are rare and an antidote is available.

Color of writing spider
The abdomen of the female is black with a whitish-yellow pattern on the sides. The legs are black with the top half orange-red. The front part of the body, the cephalothorax, is silvery-gray.

Crayfish and Crab

In the darkness of the lake bottom, beneath a flattened rock, a minor commotion was about to begin. A small crustacean, called an amphipod (am-fi-pod) or scud had just spotted a tiny (but juicy looking) crayfish peaking out from beneath a rock. Normally amphipods prefer dead meals, but perhaps a crayfish of this size would be easy prey. With its narrow back arched, the amphipod glided in to investigate. As it rounded the corner of the rock it came face to face with a very large and very protective mother crayfish. Instinctively the amphipod darted away before the mother crayfish was able to grab it with her claws. Fearing that the amphipod might try again, the mother crayfish quickly called to her young by giving off a pheromone, a chemical which has a smell that tells the young to return to their mother. To make sure that the danger signal reached all her young, she fanned the water with the legs or pleopods (plee-oh-pods) under her abdomen. Within seconds the babies were all safely clustered onto the pleopods. Then the mother turned to face the danger with her claws raised, but the amphipod did not return. The mother relaxed and her babies went back to hunting about the burrow for tiny plants, algae, and crustaceans such as daphnia and copepods.

Meanwhile, on a coastal shoreline some distance away, another crustacean was about to send her young off on their own. The female sand fiddler crab angled her way along the shore, scooping up and eating bits of plant and animal that the waves had washed in. As the sun set, she headed for the edge of the water. Then, standing with her back to the water, she gently fanned her abdomen back and forth, sending a damp flow of air over the eggs she carried beneath her. As the breeze touched them, eggs that were ready to hatch burst open, sending strange-looking young into the water.

In the morning they swam about in the plankton — the mix of fine plants and animals that floats near the ocean surface. Having survived the first month, the baby crabs molt (shed their skins) several times, their bodies grow larger and heavier, and they begin to lose their swimmerets or pleopods. After two months, their eyes and antennae are well developed and their weight causes them to sink to the ocean floor. Soon they look like small adults and join the mature crabs on the beach. But only a few make it through these many stages to return to the shore where they hatched. The others become valuable food to other creatures in the food chain of the sea.

Phylum Arthropoda
Class Crustacea
Size The average length of the freshwater crayfish is 40 to 60 mm (1.5 to 2 in); they have been known to grow up to 115 mm (4.5 in). The average fiddler crab is 38 mm (1.5 in) wide and 25 mm (1 in) long.

Distribution Crayfish are freshwater dwellers. The species in this story is found in lakes and streams from Arizona and north-central Alberta, eastward to the Atlantic Ocean. Crabs can be found in oceans throughout the world. The sand fiddler lives on protected sandy or mud beaches of marshes and tidal creeks from Cape Cod to Florida and Texas.

Food Crayfish, young and old, eat almost anything — plants, invertebrates, small fish, tadpoles, plant material. Crayfish prefer an ambush technique, they hide under a flat rock or at the entrance to the burrow. When would-be food passes by, fiddler crabs use their large claws to grab it. Food is scooped up in cup-shaped claws and shoveled into the mouth. The larvae feed on plankton near the ocean's surface.

Life History In late summer, the male crayfish moves to deeper water, makes a burrow for the female and himself, mating takes place, and the male and female stay in the burrow all winter. In April and May the female lays her eggs and secures them to the legs or pleopods on her abdomen. The male protects the female during this time, but leaves soon afterwards. The female stays in the burrow with her young. The young look like miniature adults and are ready to leave their mother's protection after their second molt (3 to 4 weeks). They will molt at least 5 times before maturity. There is one generation per year. Crayfish can live up to 4 years.

Fiddler Crabs Adult fiddlers are beach dwellers, building their burrows just below high-tide line. In mating season, the male crab digs a special burrow above high tide. He attracts a mate through a curious courtship display in which he waves his one large claw about (females do not have this large claw). After mating, the female stays in the male's burrow (under his protection) until she is ready to release her young into the ocean. Each evening she goes down to the water's edge and fans her abdomen back and forth to aerate the eggs. If an egg is ready to hatch, the shell cracks and the larva is thrown into the water. The 1 mm (.06 in) - long larva, called a zoea (zow-a), does not look at all like its parents. It will go through many different stages as a free swimming larva before taking to shore life as an adult. Maturity takes about 208 days and there is one generation per year. Maximum life span is 4 years.

Comments There is a wide variety of fascinating crustaceans living on land, in freshwater, and in saltwater. They vary in size from less than 5 mm (.2 in) in microscopic forms, to the 3.6 m (12 ft) -wide (claw to claw) Japanese spider crab. They live in many types of habitats, even in your basement (sowbugs)! Some glow in the dark, some look like tiny clams, and some live in tubes. Barnacles are also crustaceans and so are the amphipod, daphnia, and copepods in the crayfish drawing.

Color of crayfish and crab
The sand fiddler female is yellowish-gold on the upper surface with a purple patch near the eyes and reddish-brown on the sides. The zoea are sand-white in color. The crayfish is deep greenish-gold with a bit of blue. Her young are light yellowish-beige. The amphipod and copepod are yellow-beige.

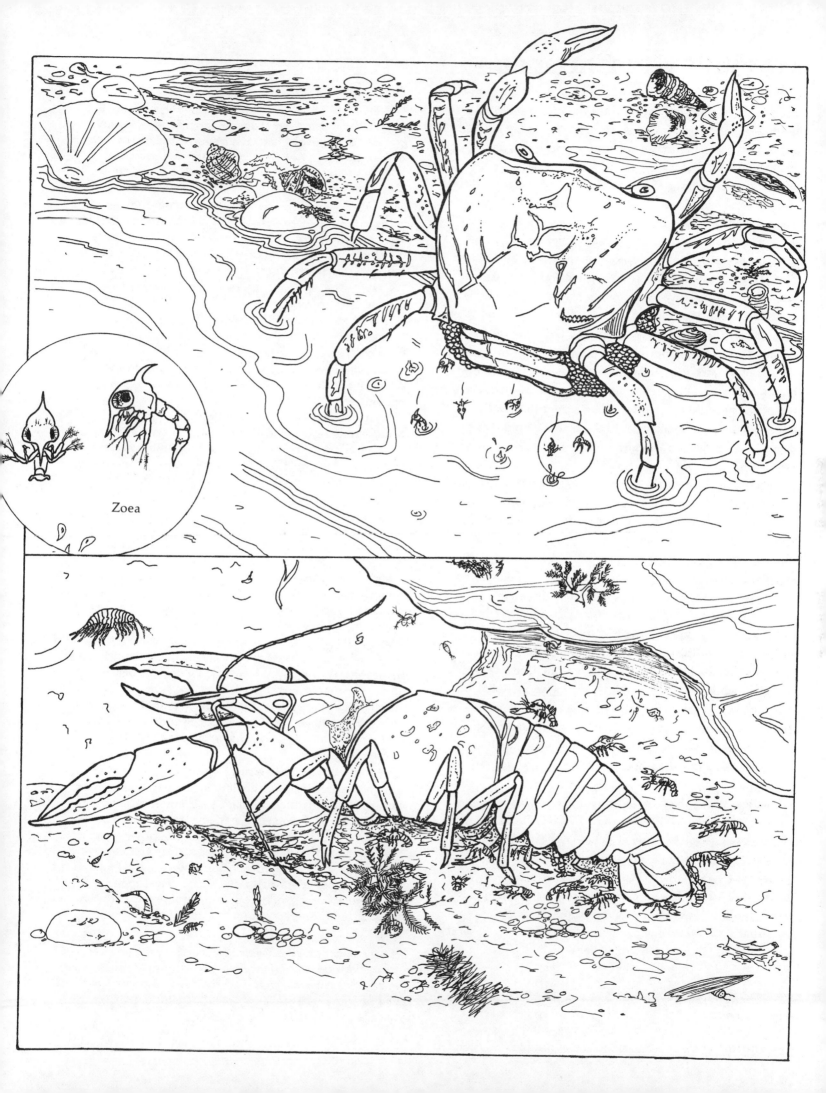

Zoea

Ant and Grasshopper

The little thatcher ant ran quickly along one of the many trails that led from the ant hill into the forest and field beyond. It had been a long summer and the young ant had done many things. She had tended the queen ant, and cleaned and fed the worm-like baby ants or larvae. She moved eggs and larvae from one chamber of the ant hill to another, and had helped create new tunnels in the nest. She went into the field following the scent trails made by other ants in her colony. Over many leaves, pebbles, and branches she searched for insects to feed to her nest mates. She gathered sweet sap from an injured tree, and even visited colonies of tiny sap-drinking insects called aphids. Thatcher ants often "milk" aphids for the sweet liquid they give. In return, the ants protect aphids from their enemies.

Now that fall was approaching, activity in the ant colony slowed more each day. Today the ant was helping her nest mates add an extra layer of twigs and spruce needles to the top of the nest. Soon, food would be harder to find, the queen would stop laying eggs, and the ants would move down into the deepest chambers of the nest to wait out the long winter season.

Meanwhile, on a sand ridge near the thatcher ant colony, another insect was getting ready for winter. She was also making a safe burrow, but the hole was not for her, it was for the pod of eggs she would soon lay. This insect was a black-winged grasshopper. All summer she had hopped from plant to plant nibbling on the juiciest leaves with her scissor-like teeth or mandibles (man-di-buls). Her keen many-lensed eyes helped her keep a careful watch for enemies. Unlike the ant who had started life as a well protected worm-like larva, the grasshopper had been on her own. She had left her egg shell looking like a very tiny, wingless adult grasshopper. Now, after several molts, and much growing, she had finally become a winged adult. Her beautiful brown wings made traveling much easier. She had moved some distance from where she had hatched.

One day she heard a wonderful song. It was made by a male grasshopper rubbing the fine combs on his legs against his wings. When she flew to find him, she discovered two male grasshoppers! When they saw her, one flew towards her. His wings softly whirred as he flew. The other male flew straight up into the air. He hovered almost two meters (6 ft) above them. "Chicka-chicka-chicka," crackled his wings. After a few seconds, he flew to a nearby grass plant. Both males were trying to get her attention. Eventually she chose one of the males as her mate. Several days later she found a site to lay her eggs.

Phylum Arthropoda

Class Insecta

Size Adult Carolina or black-winged grasshoppers measure 26 to 40 mm (1 to 1.5 in) in length from head to abdomen.

The thatcher ant queen is 20 to 27 mm (.75 to 1 in), soldier ants are 20 mm (.75 in), workers are 6 mm (.25 in) long.

Distribution Black-winged grasshoppers live in sandy, gravelly, or disturbed habitats in southern Canada (except Newfoundland) and United States south to Mexico. Thatcher ants are found in wooded areas throughout Canada and northern United States.

Food Black-winged grasshoppers eat native grasses and herbs as well as many cereal and grass-like crops. In large numbers, this insect can be a serious threat to crops. The thatcher ant's diet is extremely varied, often including plant sap, leaves, honeydew, and insects.

Life History Over the winter eggs of the black-winged grasshopper are safely buried in the soil. Being 6 mm or .2 in long at hatching in mid-May to mid-July, these tiny wingless larvae or "hoppers" spend 2 to 4 weeks eating and growing. After the fifth molt, they become winged adults. In the fall, females lay egg pods of 25 to 39 eggs, below the soil surface. The life span is one year with one generation per year.

Thatcher ants spend the winter huddled in the deepest tunnels of their ant hill. In spring, the queen begins to lay eggs while the workers look after the young, clean the nest, and gather food for the colony. Other ants, called soldiers, guard the entrances of the nest from intruders. Each ant is equipped with sharp mandibles and an irritating liquid which contains formic acid which is stored in and ejected from the abdomen. The first set of young pupate after three weeks to emerge as adult worker or soldier ants — all females. The colony continues to grow until mid-summer when special winged females and males are produced. The winged ants are not allowed to leave the nest until weather conditions are just right. Then, along with winged ants from other nearby nests, they take to the skies to find a mate. After mating, the males die; the females, now called queen ants, either return to their nest or start a new one. In new nests, the queen feeds and looks after her first brood until they mature. After that, they look after her! Thatcher ant nests often have several queens in one nest, can be 1 to 3 m (yds) high, and can be used for over 50 years. Worker and soldier ants live 1 to 3 years; queens may live 3 to 6 years.

Comments By rubbing a fine ridge of combs on their back legs against the veins on their wings, many grasshoppers make sounds that help to mark their territories and attract a mate. The grasshopper is a good example of a typical insect, having 3 body parts, 6 legs, 2 pairs of wings, and a skeleton on the outside of its body. Ants are one of the most advanced of the insects. Some species grow gardens of fungus, some raise livestock (aphids and leafhoppers) from which they harvest honeydew, and others raid other species' nests using the stolen young to serve as their slaves.

Color of ant and grasshopper
The black-winged grasshopper often matches the color of the soil where it lives. Color it light grayish-yellow, bright reddish-brown, or any shade in between. Thatcher ants have reddish-brown heads and dark brown bodies.

Sunflower Star and Purple Sea Urchin

Curled into a warm crevice of the rocky ledge a large sunflower star lazily soaked up the sun. The clear water of the tidal pool seemed to magnify the starfish's bright colors — a warning to enemies to stay away. Soon the ocean would cover the entire rock. As the tide began to rise, a shallow channel of water joined the pool with a neighboring body of water. Sensitive cells on the starfish's tube feet told it there was food in the next pool. Looking like a miniature dragon, the sunflower star gracefully glided towards the next tidal pool. As it moved, hundreds of tiny tube feet on each of its twenty-four legs took turns grasping at the rocks, pulling and pushing the starfish forward.

Meanwhile, in the next tidal pool, a purple sea urchin was using its five spike-like teeth and sharp spines to scrape and grind the rock to hollow out a pocket that would shelter it from the ocean waves. Its tube feet, which ran in five rows along its body, were attached to nearby rocks, helping it to hold its place.

As soon as the sunflower star entered the tidal pool, the sea urchin could sense that danger was near. The sea urchin immediately stopped what it was doing and began to move away. It curled its tube feet and its long spines away from the starfish, and all over its body, tiny jaw-like organs called pedicellerae (ped-i-sell-er-ay) prickled to attention, their long stalks aimed at the starfish, venom ready. The starfish raised two arms or rays and slowly scanned the pool. The simple eye on the tip of each arm told it that there were two shadows up ahead — a prickly one and a large, round one. Its keen sense of smell told it that the prickly creature was a sea urchin; the other a big juicy mussel. Although starfish will eat both, it chose to attack the mussel because it was larger and easier to handle. As it approached the mussel, it surprised a scallop hidden in the rocks. The frightened scallop clapped its shells together and quickly flipped out of reach of the starfish.

The mussel sensed danger approaching and closed its shells tightly. The starfish quickly covered it and tried to pry the shells open. Slowly it squeezed one tube foot then another into a small opening in the mussel's shells. When the opening was just one millimeter (.04 in) wide, the starfish turned its stomach outward through its mouth and squeezed one lobe into the opening. The enzymes from the starfish's stomach began to digest the clam's muscles. The prying of the tube feet tired the clam. Eventually, the starfish drew the rest of the clam's body into its own mouth to finish the meal. The starfish then turned its attention to the sea urchin. But the ocean tides had covered the pools enough so that the sea urchin had been able to escape to a safer ledge. It would not be part of the starfish's feast.

Phylum Echinodermata
Class Stelleroidea *Class* Echinoidea
Size The sunflower star is the largest sea star in the world. Its average radius is 50 cm (20 in), but it can grow to 80 cm (32 in) across. The average purple sea urchin is 10.2 cm (4 in) in width.

Distribution The sunflower star is found on rocky shores and soft bottoms from Alaska to southern California. The purple sea urchin is found on rocky shores with moderately strong surf from British Columbia to Baja California. Both species live at low-tide line and deeper.

Food The swift moving sunflower star eats clams, gastropods, crabs, barnacles, starfish, sea urchins, and occasionally algae and sponges. Sunflower stars will use their arms and tube feet to actually dig out, stone by stone, a hiding clam. While clams are pried open, sea urchins are often eaten whole! The purple sea urchin eats algae, rock-encrusting organisms, and dead animal material. The sea urchin feeds by scraping rock surfaces with one or more of its long teeth. Tiny hairs or cilia also transfer to the mouth any food particles that have landed on the sea urchin's body. In both species the mouth is in the center of the underside of the animal.

Life History *Sunflower star* Mid-May to early June, the female starfish lays up to 2,500,000 eggs. Only a few will survive, since fertilization takes place by chance meeting of the sperm and egg in the sea water. When the larvae first hatch, they are very tiny kidney bean-shaped creatures covered in cilia. The hair-like cilia help them move and catch food. As the larvae grow, the cilia decrease in number until only a band remains. Arm-like lobes begin to grow along this band of cilia. Several weeks later, 3 more arms and a central sucker develop at the other end of the larva. These arms are shorter and are equipped with sticky ends. The larva settles to the ocean floor and attaches itself by the arms and sucker. The part of the body closest to the 3 arms breaks down to form a stalk, the other part forms into a 6-armed starfish. All the adult body parts — mouth, throat, and intestine — are formed all over again. Once the tube feet and skeleton form, the 1 mm (.04 in) -wide baby starfish frees itself from its stalk and begins life on its own.

Purple sea urchin Egg production and the breeding season are similar to that of starfish. Eggs hatch within 12 hours of laying. The cilia-covered, cone-shaped larva gradually develops 5 or 6 pairs of very long thin calcium-lined arms. Each arm is lined with a row of cilia. The larva feeds on plankton for several months as its skeleton forms. Eventually the long arms are reabsorbed, and the larva sinks to the bottom to begin adult life. Sea urchins reach maturity at 2 years of age. They live 4 to 8 years and there is one generation per year.

Comments Starfish and sea urchins have an internal skeleton of calcium plates made from calcium taken from the water. Most species of starfish have only 5 arms or rays.

Color of sunflower star and purple sea urchin
The sunflower star is orange-pink with light brown patterns in the centre and along the arms. The tips of the arms are purple. The tube feet and pedicellerae (spots) are white. The purple sea urchin is a deep violet. The sea urchin's skin is dark purple to black.

Sea Cucumber

It was Maureen's first trip to the sea museum. She was looking forward to seeing all the sea creatures that would be on display. Her friend Rose was playing tour guide, since she had been there many times.

"Look at these bizarre creatures!" exclaimed Maureen.

"This is the invertebrate display," said Rose. "That pink flower-like creature is a sea anemone. And look over there. That's an ochre sea star!"

"What's hiding in that snail shell?" asked Maureen.

"It's a hermit crab. The shell is its home and its protection from enemies," explained Rose.

Nestled in a large crack in one of the rocks was an orange creature with a large fan of tentacles at one end of its body and a smaller plume at the other end. Maureen checked the sign for the creature's name.

"It's a red sea cucumber," she exclaimed out loud. "Funny, it doesn't look like a plant."

"It's not," said Rose. "It belongs to the same group as the sea stars and sea urchins."

"It says here that it feeds on tiny plants and animals that get trapped on its sticky fan of tentacles," continued Maureen.

"Look, it must be cleaning one of its tentacles right now," said Rose. As if on cue, the sea cucumber stuck one of its tentacles into its mouth.

"Sort of like licking your fingers," laughed Maureen. The girls continued to read about the sea cucumber.

"Neat," said Rose. "Its skin is different from the skin of starfish and urchins. The cucumber only has tiny plates of skeleton so its body wall is softer; plus, it has no spines, cilia, or tooth-like defense organs (pedicellerae) to protect it."

"Ooh," said Maureen, "it breathes through the bottom end of its body, not through its mouth. Its long branched lungs are called respiratory trees."

Rose groaned, "Did you read about what it does when an enemy tries to eat it? First it hides its tentacles in its mouth and as a last resort, it spits its intestines and lungs out through its back end. The enemy eats the organs and the sea cucumber sneaks away. Its organs grow back later."

"Yuk, can you imagine losing your internal organs?" said Maureen.

"Well, I guess it's better than being eaten," said Rose.

"You know, I've read that starfish can lose their arms when they get frightened," said Maureen. "They grow a new one back after a short time, and, if there is one fifth of the central disc attached to the lost arm, the arm will grow a new body too! I guess regeneration runs in the family!"

"Speaking of running, we'd better move on. There's lots more to see," said Rose. The two girls continued to other displays and other mysteries of the sea.

Phylum Echinodermata

Class Holothuroidea

Size There are about 700 species of sea cucumber in the world. They range in size from 3 cm (1.25 in) to 1 m (1 yd) in length. The average-sized red sea cucumber is 25 cm (10 in) long.

Distribution Sea cucumbers are found in oceans worldwide. The red sea cucumber is usually nestled in crevices or under rocks near low-tide and shallow waters from Alaska to the central Carolinas.

Food Red sea cucumbers (as well as most other sea cucumbers of this region) feed on small pieces of plant and animal that float by or fall onto one of its 10 highly branched tentacles. The animal keeps its tentacles clean by inserting them into its mouth to be wiped off. At the same time, the sea cucumber adds a fresh sticky coating to the tentacles to aid in food capture. When at rest, the sea cucumber keeps its body curved so that both ends — head and tail — are exposed to fresh currents of water.

Life History In late March to early May, after the first set of sunny warm days, sea cucumbers begin to spawn. First the males stretch the head end of their bodies high up from their crevices to release long plumes of pinkish-white sperm. The sperm is quickly carried away by the gentle currents of low tide. Three to 4 hours later the females begin to lay their eggs. The eggs are released from an opening at the base of the tentacles in compact pellets with over 100 eggs per pellet (a large female will produce up to 20 pellets). Soon afterwards, the pellets break up and the eggs settle to the bottom. Those that were fertilized hatch into tiny oblong cilia-covered larvae. In 2 to 3 months these larvae develop 2 or 3 long tube feet or tentacles at the bottom end and several finely branched tentacles at the mouth end. The young cucumbers settle to the bottom to find their own crevices in which to live their adult lives. It takes 2 to 3 years for sea cucumbers to reach maturity. Their life span is 3 to 7 years and there is one generation of young per year.

Comments A similar species in size, behavior, and appearance is the orange-footed sea cucumber of the east coast. When living in northern waters, this species broods its young within its body cavity.

Color of sea cucumber
The red sea cucumber is bright orange to brick red. The sponges (center right) are white, the algae below the sponges is peach colored; the sea anemones are bright pink.